Handmade
Art Nouveau Cards

Judy Balchin

D1390122

SEARCH PRESS

First published in Great Britain 2007

Search Press Limited
Wellwood, North Farm Road,
Tunbridge Wells, Kent TN2 3DR

Text copyright © Judy Balchin 2007

Photographs by Debbie Patterson and Rod Compton, Search Press Studios; and Roddy Paine Photographic Studio.

Photographs and design copyright © Search Press Ltd. 2007

ISBN-10: 1-84448-209-X
ISBN-13: 978-1-84448-209-2

The Publishers and author can accept no responsibility for any consequences arising from the information, advice or instructions given in this publication.

Readers are permitted to reproduce any of the items in this book for their personal use, or for the purposes of selling for charity, free of charge and without the prior permission of the Publishers. Any use of the items for commercial purposes is not permitted without the prior permission of the Publishers.

Every attempt has been made to contact companies who hold the copyright to the stamp and stencil designs used in this book, but in some cases this has not been possible. The authors and Publishers hope to have acknowledged all the relevant copyright holders, and to any who have been inadvertently left out we offer our sincere apologies.

Suppliers

If you have difficulty in obtaining any of the materials and equipment mentioned in this book, then please visit the Search Press website for details of suppliers: www.searchpress.com

---

Publisher's note

All the step-by-step photographs in this book feature the author, Judy Balchin, demonstrating how to make Art Nouveau greetings cards. No models have been used.

Dedication

To Miles Gardner Barrowcliffe
'I'd walk a million miles for one of your smiles!'

Acknowledgements

A big thank you to the lovely team at Search Press for their continued support and belief in me. In particular Roz Dace for her expert guidance, editor Katie Chester for her sensitive support, Juan Hayward for his wonderful design skills and Debbie Patterson, Rod Compton and Roddy Paine for their stylish photography.
Thank you to John Wright of Pebeo UK for providing the glass painting materials used in the making of this book. Also to American Traditional Stencils, Funstamps, Hampton Art Stamps, Personal Impressions, Hero Arts (©2007 Hero Arts. All Rights Reserved), Inca Stamps and Sugarloaf Inc. for permission to include rubber stamp designs to which they hold copyright.

Cover
Golden Rose project (see page 34).

Title page
Dragonflies are a popular feature of Art Nouveau designs. Here the sparkly dragonfly, jewels and gold-coloured border contrast with the muted background papers, giving the card a glitzy, vintage look.

Contents

Introduction

My love affair with the Art Nouveau period has been going on for most of my adult life, so you can imagine my pleasure when I was asked to write this book, combining it with one of my favourite crafts – cardmaking.

The French term 'Art Nouveau' means 'New Art'. It was a wonderful art movement lasting from 1880 to 1915. This short period has left us with a legacy of beautiful artworks and designs which are still used today. The artists and craftsmen of this period used organic and ornamental shapes to produce flowing, intertwining work integrating all aspects of art and design. Simple or complex, the Art Nouveau style is instantly recognisable in its balance and harmony. It arose as a reaction to the Industrial Revolution, the high level of craftsmanship contrasting hugely with the machine-made, mass-produced goods typical of the day.

My biggest challenge in writing this book was to evoke the style and colour of the Art Nouveau period using paper, card and decorative embellishments. It has been a wonderful journey and I have enjoyed every minute of it. From simple, stencilled designs, through to embellished floral designs and metal-embossed creations, glass-painted cards and stamped images – my adventure has been full of colour and texture, and totally absorbing.

I hope that you find inspiration from the techniques and ideas in this book. Use it as a launching pad for your own card creations and, most importantly, have fun!

Judy

A selection of greetings cards you can make using this book.

Materials

All of the projects in this book are created using simple techniques and materials that can be found easily in art and craft shops.

Basic materials

You will not need all of the items listed below for every project. Each project provides you with a specific materials list for you to look at before you begin.

Pencil Use this to draw lines and to trace templates.
Ruler Use a ruler to measure and draw straight lines. It is also used with the back of a scalpel to score a fold line in card.
Scalpel Use this for cutting card. Use the back of the scalpel to score fold lines in card.
Pair of compasses Draw a semicircle with a pair of compasses to create an arch shape.
Cutting mat Cut card and paper with a scalpel on a cutting mat to prevent damage to your work surface.
Scissors Round-ended scissors are used for cutting paper and card. Cutting wire can damage scissors, so use an old pair for this.
Round-nose pliers Use these for bending wire.
Ballpoint pen This is used for embossing foil.
Eyelet punch and setter Use this for punching holes in card and for attaching eyelets.

Hammer This is used with the eyelet punch and setter to attach an eyelet.

Small mat Use this when punching holes and setting eyelets to protect your work surface.

Heat tool This is used for heating embossing powders.

Fixative This is sprayed over stencilled images to prevent smudging when using chalk.

Lighter fuel Rub lighter fuel over embossed coloured foil to remove the colour from the raised areas.

Soft tissue Use this to apply the lighter fuel to the foil.

Spray adhesive This is used to glue background paper on to card.

Strong clear adhesive Use this to glue embossing foil to card and to attach craft gems and embellishments.

Masking tape Secure acetate with masking tape before painting. Also use it for securing a template to foil before embossing.

Double-sided sticky pads Sticky pads are used to attach embellishments and card shapes to the base card to give a three-dimensional effect.

Paintbrush A soft synthetic brush is used for glass painting. Use the rounded end of a paintbrush for embossing raised areas on foil.

Stencil brush Use this to apply chalks for stencilling on card.

Large soft brush Brush off excess chalk with a large soft brush, such as a make-up brush, when stencilling on card.

Palette Mix glass paints with clear medium on a palette.

Old notepad Use this as a padded surface when embossing foil.

Backing materials for card making

A huge choice of backing papers and card is now available from art and craft shops. The selection shown here includes assorted coloured card and papers, patterned background papers, handmade papers, corrugated card, watercolour paper, mirror card and embossing foils.

Glass paints, outliners and acetate

Glass paints, outliners and acetate are used to create the cards on pages 28–33. Black outliner is used for outlining the basic design on to acetate. Gold outliner is used to decorate on top of a painted design. Remember to leave the glass paints to dry thoroughly before decorating with the gold outliner.

When glass painting a design on to acetate to use in your card making, you will find it necessary to dilute some of the darker paints with clear glass painting medium to give a lighter, more pastel look. Glass paints used straight from the bottle can appear rather dark.

Punches, stencils and stamps

Keep a look out for Art Nouveau themed punches, rubber stamps and stencils at your local art and craft shops. An embossing pad and powders are used in stamp-embossing work. Coloured crayons are used to colour an embossed image. Blending chalks are used when stencilling an image.

Embellishments

Ribbons, raffia, gems, wire, eyelets, brads, skeleton leaves, readymade flowers, feathers, wooden shapes and key embellishments can all be used to decorate your cards.

Lilies and Dragonflies

As nature was the ultimate source book for Art Nouveau artists, this first project is a perfect introduction to their wonderfully organic world. The lily and dragonfly motifs were regularly used in the design of wallpaper, jewellery and furniture. Muted-coloured chalks and background papers give a more aged appearance to the card.

1 Spray the back of the butterfly paper and press it on to the front of the base card.

2 Tape the stencil on to watercolour paper and lightly draw round it with a pencil.

3 Remove the stencil. Use the stencil brush to brush the lower half of the paper with green chalks.

4 Brush the upper half with pale blue chalks.

YOU WILL NEED

Dragonfly and lily stencil

Jade green base card, cut and folded to measure 13 x 16cm (5 x 6¼in)

Jade green card, 1.5 x 2.5cm (¾ x 1in)

Heavy watercolour paper, 12 x 15cm (4¾ x 6in)

Butterfly background paper

Blending chalks

Stencil brush

Large soft brush

Two square pink gems

Green ribbon, 50cm (19¾in)

Masking tape

Double-sided sticky pad

Spray adhesive

Ruler

Scalpel

Pencil

Fixative

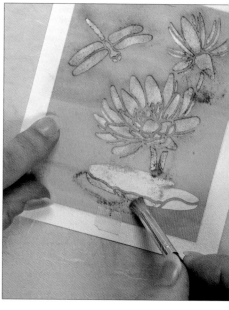

5 Replace the stencil, aligning it with the pencil lines, and attach it with masking tape. Using pink chalk, brush the ends of the dragonfly wings and petals. Shake off the excess chalk.

6 Brush the dragonfly body, wing bases and petal bases with purple chalk.

7 Brush the lily pad with light green chalk, adding dark green chalk to the leaf base and stalks.

8 Remove the stencil and brush away excess chalk dust with a large, soft brush and spray with fixative.

9 Tear round the pencilled line.

10 Lay the card on a piece of scrap paper and brush the torn edge with dark green and dark blue chalks.

11 Spray the back of the watercolour paper with glue and press it on to the base card.

12 Attach a sticky pad to the back of the small piece of green card. Remove the backing paper and press on to the watercolour paper.

13 Glue two gems to the card. Use the blunt side of a scalpel blade to help you position them.

14 Wrap the fold with ribbon and tie it in a bow at the top.

Butterflies were popular images in the Art Nouveau period. This stencilled butterfly is embellished with eyelets and a jewel to add a little sparkle.

This stencilled heart design is embellished with eyelets and a spiral of wire threaded with small key embellishments.

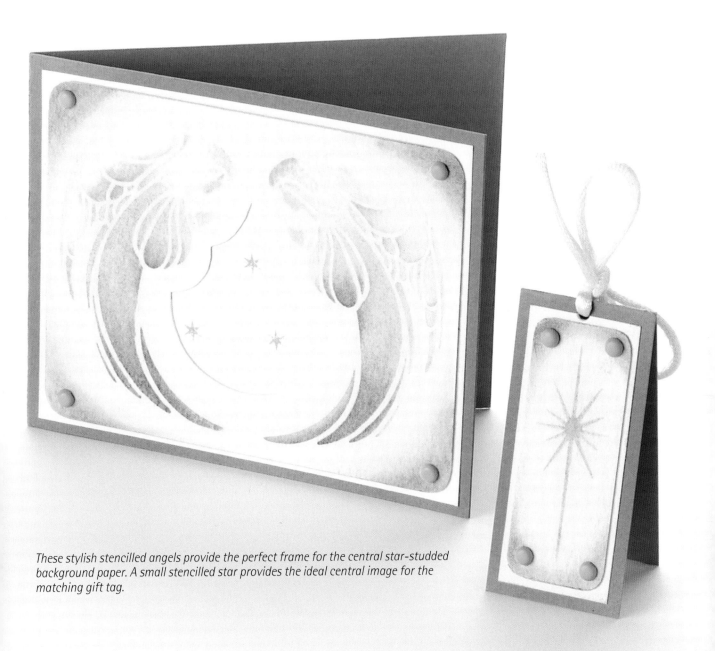

These stylish stencilled angels provide the perfect frame for the central star-studded background paper. A small stencilled star provides the ideal central image for the matching gift tag.

Rosebud Arch

Have some fun hunting down small, artificial flower embellishments to decorate your cards. Lilies and roses were used regularly in Art Nouveau arts and crafts. Soft, floral background paper and an arch of handmade paper are used to set off the delicate rosebuds. The wire stems of the rosebuds are curled to carry through the organic feel of the period.

1 Glue the background paper to the base card.

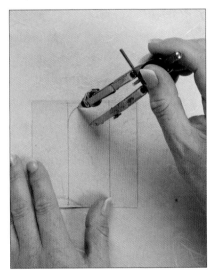

2 To create the lilac arch, draw a 4 x 9.5cm (1½ x 3¾in) rectangle on to lilac handmade paper. Use a pair of compasses to draw a semicircle at the top.

3 Cut out the arch shape.

YOU WILL NEED

Lilac base card folded to measure 9 x 20cm (3½ x 7¾in)

Lilac and blue background paper 8 x 19cm (3¼ x 7½in)

Lilac handmade paper

Pale blue card

Wooden heart embellishment painted pink

Three rosebud embellishments

Five lilac gems

Double-sided sticky pads

Spray adhesive

Pair of compasses

Pencil

Ruler

Round-nose pliers

Scissors

Scalpel

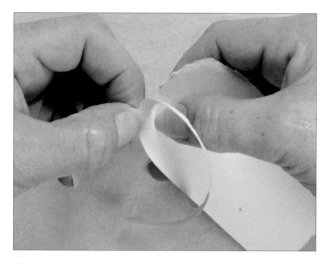

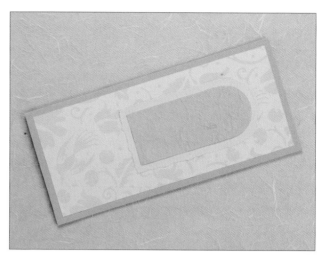

4 Draw another arch 6 x 11.5cm (2¼ x 4½in) on to pale blue card using the same technique and cut it out. Tear 0.5cm (¼in) from the edge of the card.

5 Glue the blue torn arch to the base card and the lilac arch on top.

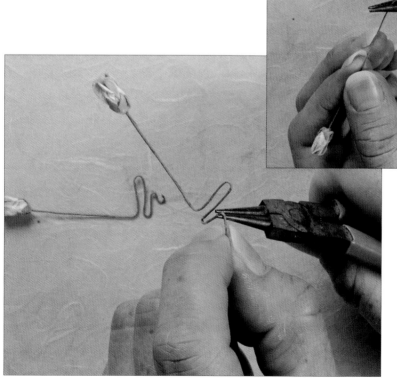

6 Create a small spiral at the end of one of the rosebud stems.

7 Bend graduating 'waves' into the ends of the other two rosebud stems.

8 Cut a sticky pad to fit across the heart embellishment and remove the backing paper.

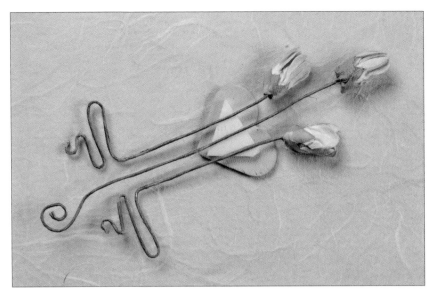

9 Lay the middle of the spiral-ended rosebud down the centre of the heart, and lay each of the remaining rosebuds on either side.

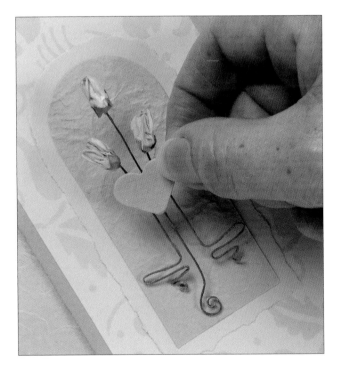

10 Press the heart on to the arch.

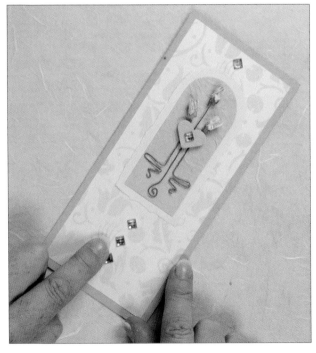

11 Decorate the heart with a gem, and glue three more gems below the arch and one above.

The antique key background paper in the card shown below left is used to link with the metal key embellishment. The stems of the lilies twine organically around the shank of the key to evoke the organic Art Nouveau style.

Foliage background paper and corrugated card are used in the card shown below right to back the delicate, intertwining lily embellishments. Simple jewels add a sophisticated touch. A matching gift tag is made using one lily. The lily stem is trimmed to fit the central panel.

A stamp-embossed border and textured handmade paper provide the perfect background for the three lilies on the card shown above left. A small wooden heart and a matching pink bow add a delicate flourish. One lily and a small ribbon bow are used to create a matching gift tag.

The floral embellishment on the card shown above right is edged with a stamp-embossed border. Deep colours are used along with the small punched dragonfly and jewel to create a truly dramatic greetings card.

Grapevine Gate Card

Metal embossing is the perfect partner for Art Nouveau designs. The unusual gate design gives a sophisticated look to this dramatic card. Coloured foil is embossed with a popular Art Nouveau grapevine design and then aged by removing the colour from the raised areas. Wrapped with ribbon and embellished with jewels, this card is perfect for any special occasion.

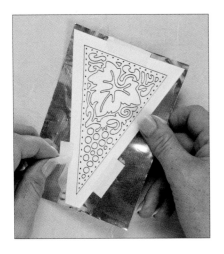

1 To make the gate card, measure and score a vertical line 5cm (2in) in from each side of the larger piece of jade card. Use the blunt edge of a scalpel.

2 Fold the flaps in and glue a strip of handmade paper to each flap.

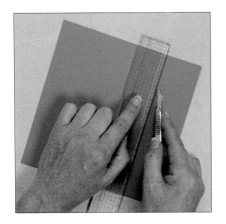

3 Tape the photocopied template to the back of the embossing foil.

YOU WILL NEED

Jade card, one 20 x 20cm (7¾ x 7¾in) and one 10 x 15cm (4 x 6in)

Pale jade handmade paper, two pieces 4 x 19cm (1½ x 7½in)

Template (see page 42)

Blue embossing foil 10 x 15cm (4 x 6in)

Ballpoint pen

Old notepad

Masking tape

Two blue gems

Blue ribbon, 1m (39½in)

Paintbrush with rounded end

Lighter fuel

Tissue

Strong glue

Spray clear adhesive

Pencil

Ruler

Scalpel

4 Working on an old notepad, trace over the design with a ballpoint pen. Press firmly to achieve a good, deep line.

5 Remove the template and work over the design once more to deepen the line.

6 Use the rounded end of a paintbrush to emboss the areas within the leaf, stems and grapes.

7 Turn the foil over. Use a tissue and lighter fuel to rub away the blue relief areas, leaving them silver.

8 Resting your work on a cutting mat, cut out the foil design using a ruler and scalpel.

9 Glue the embossed panel to the smaller piece of jade card. Cut round the card using a scalpel and ruler leaving a small border.

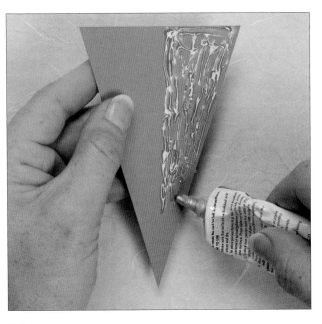

10 Turn the panel over and apply strong glue to the right-hand side.

11 With the base card face down and open in front of you, press the panel on to the edge of the right-hand flap.

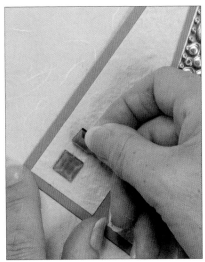

12 Close the card and decorate with the gems.

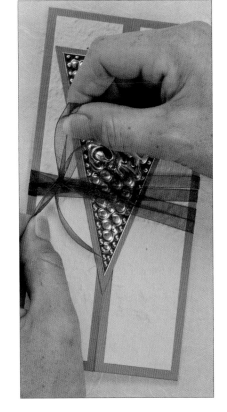

13 Wrap the card with ribbon a few times and tie in a bow.

The peacock design shown below is embossed on to silver embossing foil, cut out and backed with pastel floral background paper. It is then decorated with lilac eyelets and brads to create a simple yet effective card. A single embossed peacock feather is used to create a matching gift tag. (The templates are provided on page 43.)

For the gate card, use the project template and alternative colours and embellishments to create a totally different look. (The template is provided on page 42.)

The gold embossed roses on the card shown below left are edged with black card and crackled cream paper, then mounted on to gold card to create a sophisticated look. One embossed rose is used to create a matching gift tag. (The templates are provided on page 43.)

The popular Art Nouveau iris design shown below right is embossed on to turquoise foil. It is then cut out, glued to a gold card panel and embellished with jewels and eyelets. This panel is then glued to a base card decorated with matching handmade paper and finished with a ribbon tied at the fold. (The template is provided on page 42.)

Flower Maiden

Stylised figures were used beautifully in Art Nouveau designs. Figures, their hair and robes, were flowing and balanced. This project shows you how to translate that harmony into a card using glass paints. Remember to apply the paint liberally to achieve a flat, glass-like appearance to your image.

1 Tear across the bottom of the background paper at an angle and glue to the top of the base card.

2 Tape the photocopied template to thick white card. Tape the acetate over the template.

3 Outline the design with black outliner. The line should be even and raised, leaving no gaps.

You will need

Gold base card folded to measure 8.5 x 18cm (3½ x 7in)

Acetate 8 x 16cm (3¼ x 6¼in)

Crackled cream background paper 7.5 x 12cm (3 x 4¾in)

Thin white card 8 x 16cm (3¼ x 6¼in)

Thick white card 10 x 18cm (4 x 7in) approx.

Template (see page 44)

Black and gold glass painting outliners

Glass paints in pink, yellow, olive green and blue

Clear glass painting medium

Gold eyelet

Hole punch, eyelet setter and mat

Pink gem

Gold ribbon 25cm (9¾in)

Double-sided sticky pads

Masking tape

Spray adhesive

Small scissors

Ruler

Scalpel

4 When dry, remove the pattern. Create a flesh colour by mixing clear glass paint with a spot of yellow and pink glass paint. Paint the face.

5 Paint the hair sections with yellow paint diluted to different strengths with clear glass paint.

6 Paint the eyes blue and the leaves green.

7 Paint the lips pink. Fill in the flower petals with diluted pinks.

8 Fill in the border with pink paint and leave to dry.

9 Decorate the border with dots of gold outliner.

10 When dry, cut out the design.

11 Lay the acetate face down on scrap paper and spray it with spray glue. Press it on to thin white card.

12 Cut round the design and punch a hole in the top of the panel using the hole-punching attachment.

13 Insert an eyelet, turn the panel over and set the eyelet with the eyelet-setting attachment.

14 Thread the hole with ribbon and tie it in a bow.

15 Attach the panel to the base card with sticky pads and decorate with a gem.

The basic design for the card on the left is outlined in black on to acetate, painted and, when dry, decorated with gold outliner dots. It is then attached to the base card and decorated with gems. (The template is provided on page 46.)

The popular Art Nouveau butterfly design shown below is painted, cut out and mounted on to a base card decorated with floral background paper. Gems add a sparkle to the butterfly wings. (The template is provided on page 45.)

The tulip design above left is outlined and painted and, when dry, attached to a coloured base card. It is simple but effective. The matching gift tag is a smaller version of the card. (The templates are provided on page 44.)

The three panels of fruit on the card shown above right are outlined and painted. When dry, each is attached to a gold square of card and mounted on to foliage background paper. The panel is then attached to the base card. The matching gift tag uses a single glass-painted square. (The templates are provided on page 45.)

Golden Rose

I love stamp embossing! It is always exciting to see the embossing powders melt to create a solid image. In this project the central image is created with a rubber stamp, an embossing pad and gold embossing powder. To add subtle colour, the embossed image has been created on black card and then coloured in with pencil crayons. Backing the image with dramatic backing papers and embellishing with brads gives the whole card a rich, aged appearance.

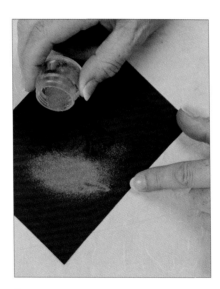

1 Press the stamp on to an embossing pad and stamp on to black card.

2 Sprinkle the image with gold embossing powder.

YOU WILL NEED

Rose rubber stamp

Rust base card folded to measure 14cm (5½in) square

Rust card 6.5 x 7cm (2½ x 2¾in)

Black card

Rust-coloured patterned background paper 13cm (5in) square

Lettered background paper 7.5 x 8cm (3 x 3¼in)

Embossing pad

Gold embossing powder

Coloured crayons, red and green

Heat tool

Hole punch, hammer and cutting mat

Four gold brads

Strong clear adhesive

Ruler

Pencil

3 Shake off the excess embossing powder on to a piece of scrap card and pour the excess back into the pot.

4 Heat the image with a heat tool.

5 Colour in the rose with a red colouring pencil.

6 Colour the leaves in green.

7 Cut round the embossed image and glue to a piece of rust-coloured card.

8 Glue the patterned background paper to the base card.

9 Glue the lettered background paper panel on top.

10 Glue the embossed image to the centre.

11 Measure and mark five equally spaced points below the panel using a pencil.

12 Punch five holes through the pencil marks.

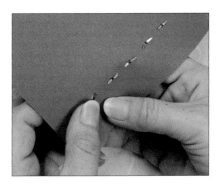

13 Insert a brad into each hole.

The central image on the card on the left is stamp embossed in copper and coloured with crayons. Butterflies punched from copper-coloured card and gold ribbons are used as embellishments to create a stylish Art Nouveau card.

The background paper on the card below is created by stamp embossing coloured leaves and small, gold dragonflies, forming the perfect background to this simple card. The tag is embellished with a dragonfly punched from gold card and tied with raffia. Make a matching gift tag by stamp embossing a single leaf and decorating with a single punched dragonfly.

Verdigris embossing powder and a small dragonfly stamp are used to decorate the crackled background paper in the card on the left. The central image is stamp embossed on to card and attached with coloured brads. A real shell adds the finishing touch.

A stylish Charles Rennie Mackintosh style stamp is used to create the central image on the card shown below right. It is then coloured with crayons, decorated with gems and cut out before mounting on to the backing card and papers. A matching gift tag is created using a smaller stamp and decorating with gems.

More ideas

There are many Art Nouveau books on the market. Look out
for Art Nouveau pattern books. Photocopy templates on to
watercolour paper and paint them. They can then be used, along
with embellishments and coloured card and background papers,
to create beautiful greetings cards like the ones shown here.

The designs below are taken from the Search Press Design
Source Books: Art Nouveau Designs and Art Nouveau Borders
& Motifs.

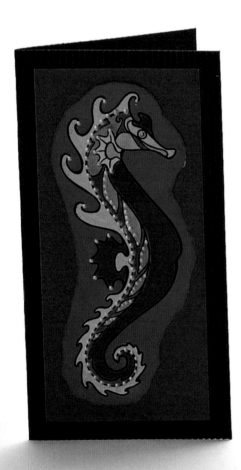

The seahorse design shown on page 40 (left) is painted using gouache to give a flat finish. It is then mounted on to card and embellished with small spots of silver outliner.

The central image on the card on page 40 (right) is painted in watercolour, cut out and mounted on to card before embellishing with a real peacock feather and a gem.

The watercoloured rose border on the card shown on the left below is enhanced with a key embellishment set against gold card.

The circular design on the card below right is watercoloured and decorated with gems and dots of gold outliner. Coloured cotton threaded with matching beads is wrapped round the fold to add a finishing touch.

Templates

All the templates required to make the cards in this book are reproduced full size on the following pages. You can also use them as a starting point for creating designs of your own. You may decide to vary the scale, using a photocopier, or to apply a different technique to create a card that is unique and personal. There are endless possibilities!

Grapevine gate card and matching gift tag, page 22

Iris design, page 27

*Peacock design, card and
matching gift tag, page 26*

*Rose design, card and matching
gift tag, page 27*

Flower Maiden, card and matching gift tag, page 28

Tulip design, card and matching gift tag, page 33

Fruit design, card and matching gift tag, page 33

Butterfly design, page 32

Maiden with hearts design, page 32

Iris design, page 48

Index

The iris flower was frequently used in Art Nouveau designs. This is translated using glass paints in this stylish glass-painted greetings card. The template is provided on page 47.